The Crisis in
Keynesian
Economics

Yrjö Waldemar Jahnsson, 1877–1936, was Professor of Economics at the Institute of Technology, Helsinki. In 1954, his wife Hilma Jahnsson established, in accordance with her husband's wishes, a foundation.

The specific purpose of the Yrjö Jahnsson Foundation is to promote economic research in Finland. To this end the Foundation supports the work of individual scholars and institutions by awarding them scholarships and grants. It also invites internationally renowned economists to Finland to give courses of lectures which are then published in this series.

YRJÖ JAHNSSON LECTURES

Kenneth J. Arrow
Aspects of the Theory of Risk-Bearing

Assar Lindbeck
Monetary-Fiscal Analysis and General Equilibrium

L. R. Klein
An Essay on the Theory of Economic Prediction

Harry G. Johnson
The Two-Sector Model of General Equilibrium

YRJÖ JAHNSSON LECTURES

The Crisis in Keynesian Economics

JOHN HICKS

BASIL BLACKWELL · OXFORD

ISBN 0 631 15500 7

Reprinted 1975

Printed in Great Britain by
The Camelot Press Ltd, Southampton

CONTENTS

PREFACE

This is a revised version of the lectures which I gave in Helsinki, at the invitation of the Yrjö Jahnsson Foundation, on 24–26 April, 1973. I am grateful for the opportunity of contributing to the distinguished series which has appeared, and will I hope continue to appear, under their auspices.

The revision has been rather considerable, particularly as regards Lecture II. Those who heard that lecture will hardly recognize the new version. As is usual with me, my thoughts develop as I am writing, and in the case of Lecture II, the development was far from complete when the lecture was delivered. What here appears has benefited from later discussions, first at Professor Paunio's seminar in Helsinki and subsequently in Uppsala, in Siena and in Oxford. To all those who took part in these discussions, and to those who have advised me respecting the less drastic revisions which I have made to the other lectures, I offer my thanks.

Oxford, July 1973

I

INTRODUCTION

The historian, for whom the second quarter of the twentieth century will be the age of Hitler, may well come to reckon the third quarter, now nearly completed, as the age of Keynes. It is true that Keynes died (in 1946) before that quarter-century opened; but it is nothing unusual for a great thinker and teacher to make his greatest impact upon the world after he is dead. That surely is what one must judge Keynes to have done.

Though Keynes wrote much about the events of the second quarter-century, and tried hard to influence them, I do not think he can be reckoned to have influenced them very much. There were many things against which he protested, and his protests against them have profoundly influenced later opinion; but the things against which he protested had usually already happened, so that it was only to a slight degree that he changed the course of events. Though it is true (to take the most important example) that the recovery from the Great Depression of 1930–2 was marked by the adoption, by several important countries, of what would now be reckoned as 'Keynesian' policies, it is rarely the case that they were consciously adopted as such.

Neither in Britain in 1931–2, in Germany in 1932–3, nor in America in 1933, was there a conscious adoption of expansionary policies in the Keynesian sense. Britain left the gold standard in 1931 because she had no alternative; interest rates were brought down to lighten the budget; the rather wild collection of measures introduced by the Roosevelt administration in April 1933, when it came into office, were obviously uninspired by any consistent doctrine. All these events, of course, precede the *General Theory* (1936). There was no time for the teaching of that book (generally regarded nowadays as incorporating the essential Keynesian doctrine) to make a deep impression on any but professional economists before the war began. It was during the war, and immediately afterwards, that people who had had time to absorb that doctrine began to come into positions of authority. Thus it is at the end of the war (which, economically considered, was hardly before 1950) that the age of Keynes, in practice, begins.

For at least half of the twenty-five years that I have attributed to it, it must be judged to have been a great success. Those who look for *long waves* in economic affairs will surely judge the 1950s, and most of the 1960s, to have been a prolonged boom. As with former long booms of such character, it was not uninterrupted by checks, or recessions; but the recessions were shallow and brief. There were many good years and they were very good years; there were few bad years and they were not very bad. What a contrast with the years between the wars, when the good years were scarce, while the bad years were many and very bad!

It does, however, remain an open question how far this success was due to Keynesian policies. The boom was nearly universal but the Keynesian policies were by no means universal. It may, however, well be argued that they were sufficiently general to cause a general expansion; those who took no active part were yet borne up on the expansion engineered by others. But even if that is granted, it does not dispose of the alternative view. The combination of more rapid technical progress (surely a fact) with the socialist tendencies which increased demand for collective goods (surely also a fact) could have produced such a boom without the added stimulus of Keynesian policies. It is still unclear how much is to be attributed to the one and how much to the other.[1]

There can yet be no doubt that the boom was associated, in the minds of many, with the Keynesian policies; so when, at some date in the late sixties (varying from country to country), the boom itself began to falter, the authority of the policies that were supposed to have led to it inevitably began to be called in question. Instead of producing *real* economic progress, or growth, as they had for so long appeared to do, they were just producing inflation. Something, it seemed clear, had gone wrong.

What was it? That is a major question, one of the largest questions with which the world is at present confronted; I do not suppose that I am able to answer it. So I shall con-

[1] For an important study of this matter with respect to the particular British case, see R. C. O. Matthews, 'Why has Britain had Full Employment since the War?' *Economic Journal*, September 1968.

fine myself in these lectures to a subsidiary matter, of much interest in itself, on which I may be able to throw some light.

It is by no means surprising—it is indeed very natural—that when the time came for the Keynesian policies to yield, or to appear to yield, less satisfactory results, they, and their intellectual basis, should be called in question. That is what happens in all human affairs, in politics, in religion and in morals, as well as in economics. As in these other cases, the questioning takes various forms. It is unnecessary to go to the extreme of maintaining that the established doctrine is just wrong; it is easier to claim that it has been wrongly interpreted. But once it is granted that one wrong interpretation is possible, the way is open for the discovery of other wrong interpretations; and for competing views about right interpretations. So the issue which seemed closed is reopened. We have to start, in a way, all over again.

In the case of Keynes, one can see just this happening. The range of interpretation is widening out, and doctrines which look very different from what was orthodox Keynesian economics are claiming a place under the Keynesian umbrella.[2] And indeed in the case of Keynes it is very easy. For Keynes was a man of extremely active mind, whose thinking never stayed still but was always pushing on. Some of those who worked with him could not

[2] I think, of course, in the first place of Milton Friedman and his 'Quantity Theory' followers; but there are several writings by others which appear in a collection such as R. W. Clower's Penguin *Readings in Monetary Theory*, London, 1969, which would answer to the same description.

stand the pace: 'you never knew what he would be saying next'. Even his greatest book, *The General Theory of Employment*, is by no means wholly self-consistent; and much of it appears inconsistent with other writings, which themselves contain ideas which do not seem to have been abandoned. Besides, he lived for ten years after the publication of the *General Theory*; and there is plenty of evidence that in those years, as one would expect, he was still pushing on. So the content of what really is Keynes's own doctrine, Keynes's own version of Keynesian economics, is by no means easy to determine.

I do not pretend that I can determine it; yet on these matters I think I have something to say. It will be fair, before proceeding, to explain my personal position.

There are several economists still living—Richard Kahn, Joan Robinson, Roy Harrod and James Meade—who, in the critical years when the *General Theory* was forming, were members of Keynes's own circle. Each of them, we now know, took some part in the making of the book. I was not a member of that group. I never met Keynes until the book was almost completed, though I had some correspondence with him before that.[3] I was working at the London School of Economics, which had the reputation of being a stronghold of 'anti-Keynesianism'; and when I wrote my first book, *The Theory of Wages* (1932), I was a regular member of the LSE group. I was, however, 'converted'; or rather, I may claim, I converted myself. Within

[3] I have published some of this correspondence in 'Recollections and Documents', *Economica*, February 1973.

months of the publication of my *Wages* book, I was writing papers which diverged from the regular LSE line; and by the end of 1934, when my ideas were more formed, I was publishing things which were recognized by Keynes (in correspondence) as being more on his side than on the other. It was only one part of the Keynesian system on which I had got my hand; but it was enough to make a great deal of difference to one's attitude towards economic problems. So it was no doubt because of the attitude which I was known to be taking up that I was asked to review the *General Theory*, when it appeared, for the *Economic Journal* (the journal of which Keynes himself was principal editor). I was asked because it was hoped that I should be a sympathetic but independent critic; and such, at that date, were not easy to find.

I had little time to write that review; so I was not (and am not) very satisfied with it. Only a few months later I felt that I must do it again. The result was the paper 'Mr. Keynes and the Classics'[4] with the SILL diagram that has got into so many text-books. To many students, I fear, it *is* the Keynes theory. But it was never intended as more than a representation of what appeared to be a central part of the Keynes theory. As such, I think it is still defensible.[5] But I have never regarded it as complete in itself. In fact, only two years later, in *Value and Capital* (1939), I myself put

---

[4] Published in *Econometrica*, 1937; reprinted in my *Critical Essays in Monetary Theory*, 1967, and often elsewhere.

[5] It would appear that Keynes himself accepted it as such. See his letter of March 1937, printed in my 'Recollections and Documents' (cited above), and also in Keynes, *Works* XIV, 79–81.

forward what is surely a very different formulation. This also has had much effect; the version of Keynes that is put forward in many modern writings (especially, perhaps, those descended from Patinkin[6]) looks to me more like the *Value and Capital* formulation than like Keynes's own. So that also, in what follows, will require some attention.

But that, of course, is by no means all. There have been later works, of which Metzler's 'Three Lags in the Circular Flow of Income'[7] and Harrod's *Dynamic Economics* seem to me to have been particularly important, which (while remaining strictly within the Keynesian tradition) have opened up new vistas beyond those directly contemplated by Keynes. My own *Contribution to the Theory of the Trade Cycle* (1950) belongs to that group; it may be regarded as an attempt to do for them what SILL had done for the *General Theory* itself. But in formalizing their work, it raised further issues, of which I myself became conscious only gradually. It was only while writing *Capital and Growth* (1965) that I began to realize that, as a consequence of what had happened, the *General Theory* itself needed considerable reconstruction.

What I shall try to do in the following is some of that reconstruction. Though it sounds a hard task, it is in fact rather easy. For what results is not far from what is implicit in the work of practical economists at the present time. When I read the surveys of the wiser economic commen-

---

[6] *Money, Interest and Prices*, 1956, 1965. Several of the papers in the Clower readings (cited above) answer to this description.

[7] In *Essays in Honour of Alvin Hansen*, New York, 1948.

tators, I recognize that much of what I shall be saying is well known to them; they have been finding it out by experience. It is nevertheless possible that it may be of use to them—and should certainly be of use to students, who will be the economic commentators of the next generation —to have it set out in fairly formal terms. Economics, Keynes himself said, is a 'technique of thinking'; perhaps it is just as important that it is a language—a means of communication. A theory which is up-to-date—which does not forget the most pressing problems of the present day— should make communication easier. It is something of that sort which by my reconstruction I hope to achieve.

As is indicated, quite correctly, on the SILL diagram, the Keynes theory falls into three parts. Taking them in Keynes's own order, there is (1) the effect of investment on income and employment—the Multiplier theory, (2) the effect of interest on investment—the Marginal Efficiency of Capital, and (3) the effect of money supply, or of monetary policy, upon the rate of interest—Liquidity Preference. I shall follow that order, and shall thus begin with the Multiplier.

SAVING,
INVESTMENT AND THE
MULTIPLIER

On the simplest—and crudest—version of the multiplier theory, income (which governs employment) is determined from investment quite mechanically. Saving and investment are always equal. There is a relation between income and consumption—the consumption function—which is taken as given. Since saving is the difference between income and consumption, saving is similarly a function of income. It is a function which is capable of being inverted, so as to show income as a function of saving. Thus with given investment, and so given saving, income is determined; and employment is determined from income.

To this simple version there are two qualifications, already mentioned—indeed emphasized—by Keynes. In order that the consumption function should be such that it can reasonably be expected to remain stable over time, it must be measured in wage-units; that is to say, in money values deflated by an index of money wages. Only if money wage-rates are constant is it proper to measure it in money terms. I shall return to this question later;[1] for the moment

[1] See below, pp. 59–61.

I shall suppose that money wages do remain constant, since there are other matters which require attention before we come to wages.

Secondly, it was admitted that a consumption function, which is to be stable over time, cannot express a relation between income and saving which is to hold whatever they are; it must express a relation between *normal* income and *normal* saving. And it is impossible, after a disturbance (such as an unexpected increase in investment), that income and saving can at once become normal; they can only become normal after a lapse of time. So the multiplier is not instantaneous; it takes time to operate. An initial increase in investment raises incomes in the investment goods producing industries; the spending of these additional incomes raises incomes in consumption goods producing industries; the spending of these raises incomes in other consumption goods producing industries; and so on. As Kahn had shown, this process is a convergent process; but it is a process—it cannot take place all at once. All, therefore, that can be read off from the consumption function is an equilibrium to which the system is tending. So long, however, as the convergence is fairly rapid that may be good enough.

Nothing much (so far) stands in the way of the practical application which Keynes of course had in mind. Investment (he was never tired of insisting) is a flighty bird, which needs to be controlled; but if we can find a way of regulating it, through the rate of interest or otherwise, the rest of the economy will look after itself. This implies, it will be noticed, that the money wage-level is not de-stabilized; it is assumed that there is a good deal of 'play' before that happens. But I am leaving that question until later; for there is another difficulty, which emerges as soon as the multiplier analysis is looked at more closely, which is at least in part independent of any unsettlement of wages.

It is easiest to see it by taking an example. Suppose that investment expenditure is raised, by some act of policy, above what it would have been otherwise; and that it is maintained at this higher level for some considerable time. Let us say that this additional investment takes the form of building houses. You cannot build houses without materials, which (for brevity) I will call bricks. In order that labour should be employed in building houses, bricks must be available. If we try to increase employment in house-building at a time when all bricks that are currently being produced by the brickmakers are already being used, we cannot do it—unless there are stocks of bricks on which we can draw. But suppose that the bricks are in fact acquired by drawing on stocks. While that is happening, the actual increase in investment will be less than the new investment expenditure by the house-building industry; for the expenditure on bricks by that industry is offset by disinvestment in the stock of bricks. There is net additional investment to the extent of the additional labour employed by the building industry, but no more than that. And in order that there should be even that, there must have been stocks of bricks on which to draw.

Now it is of course true that as the brickmakers find their stocks of bricks diminishing, they must in the end take steps to expand their output of bricks. But there is no firm rule just when this will happen, or to what extent it will happen. The decision by the brickmakers to expand output is itself an investment decision, which is not tied down to a particular date or to a particular amount. Some of what Keynes was saying about the flightiness of investment applies here too. It is surely wrong to take reinvestment for granted, as Keynes, in so much of his work, appears to have taken it.[2]

It is important to be clear just what this consequential

---

[2] There is something here which is very curious. In the *Treatise on Money* Keynes gave much attention to working capital, and to 'liquid capital' (i.e. stocks); but in the *General Theory* they have nearly disappeared. He had evidently convinced himself, by the work which he had done in the *Treatise*, that they do not matter. They are merely a reflection of 'output', which is governed by effective demand. 'The decline in output brought a disinvestment in working capital', as he put it himself in a passage that comes to hand, written in 1931 (*Works* XIII, 351).

Did he get into the habit of thinking in this way, because he had begun with 'output' expressed in monetary, or value, terms, and with markets behaving in a Marshallian—or what I shall be calling a flexprice—manner? On that interpretation, a fall in demand *immediately* results in a fall in 'output', i.e. value of output, which transmits itself to a fall in the value of working capital. But if one is thinking in real terms—and by the time he came to the theory of employment he should have been thinking in real terms—the causation is surely the other way about. A fall in demand may indeed reduce sales; but real working capital (i.e. goods in process) must be reduced before output (physical output) is reduced. Stocks may indeed pile up at any stage of the process; but surplus stocks should surely not be regarded as part of real working capital. It makes for confusion so to regard them; a confusion which (as we shall see) is much more serious in the case of expansion in final demand than in the case of decline.

What exactly happened to Keynes's thinking at this point deserves more consideration than I have been able to give it; now that the papers relating to the *General Theory* have been published (*Works* XIII–XIV) it should be possible to clear the matter up. It seems to me to be rather fundamental.

rise in output implies. It could be that the rise in brick out-put, when it comes, is no more than sufficient to stop the fall in the stock; the stock of bricks will thereafter be maintained, but it will be maintained at a lower level than when the process began. If this happens, the net investment in house-building (taking brick-using and brick-making together) will rise towards the figure set by the original additional investment expenditure in house-building, since the use of bricks by the builders is no longer offset by the fall in stocks. (I say 'rise towards', since we must not forget the use of materials by the brick-making industry. If the makers of these materials react similarly, the increase in investment due to the additional house-building will ultimately rise to equal the original increase in investment expenditure; but one can see that it may take quite a long time for this to happen.)

So far, however, this is a convergent series, like the Kahn multiplier; it may be regarded as a gradual rise in the multiplicand, to which the rising multiplier is applied. It is an additional reason why the response of employment to a change in investment expenditure may be lagged. But more is involved than just a deferment of the date at which the final equilibrium is reached. At every stage in the process just described, there will have been a fall in stocks. At the end of the sequence they will have stopped falling; but they will stand at a lower level than that at which they would have stood if the rise in investment expenditure had not occurred.

I have so far followed out the sequence in terms of the

stages of production of investment goods; but there will be a broadly similar sequence on the side of consumption goods also. So it is not just the multiplicand which is affected; the multiplier is affected also. As the builders, initially drawn into employment, spend their wages, the first thing that happens is that stocks of consumption goods in the shops are reduced. This also, as it occurs, must be counted as dis-investment. Because of this disinvestment, which must be set off against the original rise in investment, the spending of the increased wages does not, for some time, exercise its full effect on employment.

I have insisted that the response of producers to changes in stocks is an investment decision; so it depends on informa-tion, and on state of mind. It is conceivable—just conceiv-able—that all the responses (and, as we have seen, there are many responses at many stages that are in question) may be very fast, perhaps so fast that many decisions to start new production of materials and consumption goods, at various stages, are made at the moment when the original invest-ment expenditure begins. But it would be very surprising if this should happen. The evidence seems to be that the lag is usually quite considerable; the fall in stocks must therefore be considerable too.

But there cannot be a fall in stocks unless there are stocks to fall. Thus it is impossible to tell the multiplier story properly in terms of the *flow* relations between income and saving, to which Keynes (in the main) confined himself. The state of stocks, even the initial state of stocks, must be considered too.

It has become conventional (since the time when it was recognized that the level of stocks must not be neglected) to suppose that it is regulated by what is called the *stock adjustment principle*. Producers (and traders) are supposed to have some desired level of stocks; so their demand for replacements is governed, in the first place, by the rate of sales which they expect, and in the second place by the difference between actual stock and desired stock. It is not supposed that they will seek to reach their desired stock instantaneously; they will plan to work up their stocks, or to work them down, over an appreciable period. It is further assumed that the desired stock has some relation to current output; but here again it is unreasonable to suppose an immediate reaction. A change in the rate of sales must be supposed to exhibit some degree of persistence, before it changes the desired stock.

Assumptions such as these are convenient for mathetical manipulation. When they are applied to the multiplier story, they generate sequences which are not hard to work out. It is necessary to stipulate what is the state of stocks when the story begins. If, at the moment when investment expenditure is stepped up, the level of stocks is normal (actual stock = desired stock), the fall in stocks, which has been described, must make actual less than desired. There will then, according to the assumption, be at some point a positive investment in stocks, not hitherto taken into account. If there were no such *induced investment*, outputs of materials (and of consumption goods) rising no further than was necessary to stop the fall in stocks, the system would come into equilibrium, after a time, with actual net investment increased to the full extent of the initial increase in investment expenditure, and with a rise in income exactly as shown in the *simple* Keynes model; a normal multiplier being applied to the initial increase in investment expenditure. But if there is this induced investment, output will expand beyond the point that is shown in the simple Keynes model; as I said in my book on the *Trade Cycle* (1950) there is a super-multiplier.

I need not repeat the story of the super-multiplier. Its tendency to produce fluctuations, of the type of the 'inventory cycles' which seem to occur in practice, is well known. It is more to the point, for my present purpose, to observe that the stock adjustment assumptions, in the form in which they lead to the inventory cycle, are not the only possible assumptions. There are other cases, at least equally plausible; and some of these appear equally recognizable in practice.

First of all, it is not necessary (even on stock adjustment assumptions) that we should begin with normal stocks. It might happen, at the moment when the new investment expenditure was undertaken, that actual stocks were greater than desired stocks. The fall in stocks, which occurred in the working out of the multiplier process, might then do no more than absorb these surplus stocks. Though it would still take time for the multiplier to work out its full effect, the level of stocks at the end of the process would be more normal than it was; not only in the flow sense but also in the stock sense there would have been a movement towards equilibrium. The general impression that is given by

Keynes's account would then be entirely correct. It will, however, be noticed that in this case, when there are surplus stocks in the initial position, there would have been a tendency to contraction in the initial position—a tendency which the expansion in investment expenditure (as on house-building) would have tended to correct. The expansion in investment would have arrested a decline; so it is not surprising that it should be stabilizing. Now this, as a matter of history, was surely the situation with which Keynes was confronted at the time his ideas were forming. His prescription, and the theory which he developed to justify it, do in that case fit.[3]

And there is a further, more general, point, which tends the same way. The stock adjustment principle, with its *particular* desired level of stocks, is itself a simplification. It would be more realistic to suppose that there is a range or interval, within which the level of stock is 'comfortable', so that no special measures seem called for to change it. Only if the actual level goes outside that range will there be a reaction. It would then be possible, if the original expansionary programme were fairly modest, for there to be no induced investment in stocks, even if initial stocks were normal. At the end of the process, stocks would indeed be reduced; but they would still be within the range.

[3] But see preceding note. Keynes was very well aware that surplus stocks are a depressive factor. He had been into this in Chapter 29 of the *Treatise*; he emphasized it, subsequently, again and again. That must surely be admitted; but it seems to have obscured in his mind the other important fact that some degree of 'ease' in the stock situation is a necessary condition for real expansion, even expansion of employment, if that is to proceed at all smoothly.

Nevertheless, as we move towards realism, we must surely go further. As we saw, in our first discussion of house-building, there are many stages of production, with corresponding stocks, that are involved. These will, in general, be stocks of physically different kinds. There is no reason why the relation of *actual* to *desired*, whether *desired* is tightly or loosely interpreted, should be the same in each case. There will ordinarily be some stocks that are in ample supply and some that are scarce.

It is of vital importance, when we proceed to discuss these differences in stock situation, to distinguish between the case of a closed economy, with no external trade, and an open economy, which is engaged in international trade. Though the principles are the same, the way in which the process appears to work is very different. I begin with the case of the closed economy.

We know what happens in the closed economy from wartime experience. The shortages of particular materials cause 'bottlenecks'. If (as in the example from which I started) there are no surplus stocks of bricks, there can be no extra house-building, and no extra employment on house-building, until extra bricks have been produced. If there are ample materials for producing bricks, the extra bricks can be produced, but only after a delay. If there are not ample materials for producing bricks, these also have to be produced, and the delay is longer. The bottlenecks slow up the expansion in output, and also in employment.

It would indeed seem to be quite difficult, if the shortage of materials is at all widespread, for the 'Keynesian' expansion to get started, except on a very limited scale. Something can be done by employing labour directly, without materials; but an expansion which is limited to a demand for personal services is a miserable substitute for the general expansion which Keynes seemed to promise. Industrial processes appear to require materials *at every stage*. Though it is sometimes useful, for theoretical purposes, to postulate a 'beginning' which requires no more than direct labour, such a 'beginning' is in fact hard to find. If there are no materials which can be drawn into the productive process (no surplus stocks of the most essential materials) it must be hard to get an industrial expansion started at all.

But even so there is a way out. The *particular* new investment activity (in our example, the house-building) which I began by introducing, can still be started, and developed, if the requisite materials can be drawn from other industries. These may be investment goods industries, or they may be consumption goods industries. If the materials are drawn from the former, one form of investment is expanded at the expense of another; so it is uncertain whether, on balance, investment will be expanded or not. If they are drawn from the latter, there will have to be a *real* contraction in consumption—when the multiplier (so it appeared) was calling for a rise! But in fact, if materials are withdrawn from consumption goods industries (which, it will be remembered, we are assuming to have no surpluses of materials) both the output of those industries and employment in those industries must decline. So it is again by no means certain that there will be a net expansion in employment. There will just be a transfer of activity from one industry to another; the rise in the one may be greater than the fall in the other, or it may be less.

This is of course what used to be said by those official economists in England, on whose 'Treasury View' Keynes made so devastating an attack. I have no doubt at all that in the circumstances of that time, Keynes was entirely right. What I have sought to show is that the rightness of Keynes's contention depended upon the availability of stocks of materials, which could be drawn upon without disrupting other economic activities. The existence of such stocks, in the practical case, was the thing which the official economists overlooked.

I turn to the open economy, where the problem, at first sight, looks so much easier. For by trade with the outside world particular bottlenecks can usually be relieved. If the materials needed for the expansion are not available at home, they can be imported. For most sorts of materials (in the widest sense of materials) this, for the national economy, is much the easiest way out. Materials are imported, and additional consumption goods also are imported —when the additional demand for consumption goods, generated by the muliplier, cannot conveniently be met from home production. Both from increased imports, and (sometimes) from diminished exports, the additional goods are drawn in, without disrupting any part of the domestic productive process.

So the problem (as we are all by this time well aware) becomes a problem of the balance of payments. We are used to thinking of it in those terms; what I want to emphasize here is that it is simply a variant on the closed economy problem which we have just been discussing. We may look upon the country's stock of foreign exchange as one kind of reserve stock, available to play the same part as the physical stocks, which were the only kind of reserve which could be available in the closed economy. The open economy has, or may have, this additional stock; and it is in fact the easiest of all stocks on which to draw. But it is of course not inexhaustible. So, as in the case of the physical stocks of the closed economy, it makes a great deal of difference whether the stock of foreign exchange is large or small, at the time when the expansion in employment starts.

I do not think it is necessary for me to re-tell the story in balance-of-payments terms, for in that form it is familiar enough. It is perfectly possible for the reserves of foreign exchange that are drawn on at an early stage of expansion, to be replenished at a later stage by the working of a 'super-multiplier'—just like the stocks of physical goods in a closed system. But we have now had plenty of experience of the less favourable alternative—attempts at expansion which have been cut short by balance-of-payments crises. In my own country this has happened several times, but we still find it hard to learn from experience. What is particularly serious for us (and for anyone else who ventures to try the experiment) is that other people learn. The reserve of foreign exchange, on which we can draw, is not accurately measured by the reserve of the Central Bank. It is mainly a matter of the network of debts and credits owed to and from abroad—and that is a flighty bird, if ever there was one! There may seem at one moment to be an adequate reserve; then, by failure of confidence, it may vanish overnight. Thus while reliance on imports seems an easy way of supporting an expansion, it is a prop which one may suddenly find to have been removed.

It will no doubt be expected that I should go on, at this point, to discuss the burning question of fixed versus flexible exchanges. But before I come to that I need further preparation. A change in the rate of exchange is a change in prices; and on prices, in general, I have so far had nothing to say. It will be useful to give some attention to the role of prices, in a closed system, before considering what may happen, in an open system, with flexible exchanges.

In discussing the multiplier theory without attention to prices, I am following a precedent set by a great part of Keynesian literature. It is practically taken for granted, in many expositions, that there are just two causes of changes in prices: changes in real costs (technical progress) and changes in money wages. The former of these, during the time that is taken for the multiplier to work out, is taken to be negligible (though when we stretch out the multiplier process, in the way that we have seen to be necessary, this may be doubted). As for money wages, they may indeed rise from shortage of labour, as full employment is reached; and they may also rise for what is regarded as an independent or exogenous cause—wage-push by trade unions. The latter is indeed a complication, but (so we are given to understand) it has nothing to do with the multiplier process itself.

I have myself described the analysis which proceeds on these lines as *fixprice theory*[4]—using that term to mean, not that prices do not vary, but that the causes of their variation are outside the model. So we suspend the rule that price must change whenever there is an excess of supply or excess of demand. I do not at all deny that this fixprice assumption is a useful assumption, up to a point—but only up to a point. (That, I believe, is the most it can have been for Keynes himself. He had far too much experience of speculative markets to swallow the fixprice assumption whole.)

The fact surely is that in modern (capitalist) economies there are, at least, two sorts of markets. There are markets where prices are set by producers; and for those markets, which include a large part of the markets for industrial products, the fixprice assumption makes good sense. But there are other markets, 'flexprice' or speculative markets, in which prices are still determined by supply and demand. It is tempting, when one is constructing an economic model, to simplify by assuming just one sort of market. Thus one may assume that all markets are fixprice markets, and get a fixprice theory; or one may assume that all markets are speculative markets. The latter is a less popular alternative, but theories of that type can be, and have been, produced. One of them is the theory that I myself produced in *Value and Capital*.[5]

[4] *Capital and Growth*, Chapter 7.
[5] See especially Parts III and IV of that book.

A pure flexprice theory, of that type, is not realistic, though it may be instructive. It is doubtless less realistic than a pure fixprice theory. But a pure fixprice theory is itself not wholly realistic. For speculative markets (such as markets for staple commodities, not to speak of financial markets) do exist.

What we need is a theory which will take account of both sorts of markets, a theory in which both fixprice and flexprice markets have a place. Why some sorts of commodities should be traded on one sort of market and some on the other is an interesting question; but I shall leave it to one side. I will merely observe that in a fixprice market, the stocks that are held will be held by firms that are specialized, either to the selling or to the buying of the commodity in question; there will be no intermediate traders (or, if there appear to be such, they are effectively under the control of seller or buyer). It is characteristic of a flexprice market, on the other hand, that there exist intermediate traders—independent intermediate traders—traders who will, on occasion, either buy or sell.

One of the most important things which we have learned from Keynes is that prices, in a flexprice market, though they appear to be determined by current demand for the commodity and new supplies coming forward, are in reality determined by the willingness of traders to hold stocks. The equilibrium of the market is a stock equilibrium, not a flow equilibrium. Though Keynes made the point (in the *General Theory*) chiefly with reference to financial markets, it is clear that it holds quite generally—for all markets in which there is holding of stocks.[6] It is natural to think of such a market as being in equilibrium when the only transactions that are occurring are sales to buyers going outside the market and purchases from sellers coming from outside the market; and when those purchases and sales are in balance. But all that is signified by such outside sales and purchases being in balance is that the stocks which are held in the market (that is to say, by the intermediate traders) are unchanged. The question still arises: will the price that keeps outside supply and demand in balance be such that the traders will be willing to leave their stocks unchanged? If, at that price, they desire to increase their stocks, the actual price must rise above the flow equilibrium price. The market will find a temporary equilibrium, at a price which makes outside demand less than outside supply—the difference being made up by an addition (a desired addition) to traders' stocks.

The major difference between the working of a fixprice market and that of a flexprice market now becomes apparent. In the fixprice market (as we have seen) actual stocks may be greater, or may be less, than desired stocks; in the flexprice market, on the other hand, actual stocks are always equal to desired stocks—when the stocks of the traders are taken into account. But what then corresponds to the disequilibrium which (as we have seen) can so easily arise on the fixprice market? There must be something in the flexprice market that corresponds.

[6] Flexprice markets in which there is no holding of stocks are very exceptional—in the real world, though not in economic text-books!

One cannot answer that question without asking why the traders should hold stocks. The obvious answer is that they must expect to make a profit from doing so; and that seems to mean that they must expect to sell at a higher price than that at which they have bought. This cannot, however, be the whole answer; for it would imply as soon as the current price had reached what was thought to be a normal level, so that there was no expectation of a further rise, stocks would vanish; and that hardly agrees with observation. Some allowance must clearly be made for uncertainty of price-expectations, in order to get a proper account of the working of such a market. We may nevertheless get a fair approximation if we think of the traders requiring to keep some minimum stock in order to stay in business; this would correspond to the 'normal stock' of the fixprice market. If outside supply became greater than outside demand, the difference would be absorbed by traders, thus moderating the fall in price which would otherwise occur; but it would be necessary, in order that they should act in this way, that the price should fall below 'normal', the extent of the fall being largely determined by the costs of holding the surplus stocks.[7] If, at a later date, outside supply fell short of outside demand, the stocks would be re-absorbed, and the price would return towards normal. But if an excess demand appeared when there were no surplus stocks in this sense, the extent to which traders would be willing to use their stocks to moderate the rise in price would not be considerable. They might well do so, if the shortage

[7] See again Chapter 29 of the *Treatise on Money*.

was expected to be very temporary; but not otherwise.

Let us go back to the multiplier. We have seen, when discussing the multiplier in fixprice terms, that a smooth expansion, of the kind Keynes envisaged, requires the presence of surplus stocks, at least to some degree. So far as the fixprice commodities are concerned, what was formerly said continues to hold. So far as the flexprice commodities are concerned, the corresponding condition is that prices should be abnormally low. They must be abnormally low, not just in the sense that they look low on a statistical time-series; they must be thought to be abnormally low, so that there is an expectation of recovery, at the least a good chance of recovery. From that situation, an actual increase of effective demand will induce a rise in the prices of flexprice commodities—a rise towards normal. In terms of prices, as in terms of quantities, the movement (beginning from surplus stocks) is a movement towards equilibrium.

What will be the effect on the prices of fixprice commodities? The fixprice commodities, as we have defined them, are not to be supposed to have prices that are fixed, whatever happens; they are characterized, not by that, but by some degree of insulation from the pressures of supply and demand. If their costs of production rise, their prices may well rise; if their costs fall their prices may also fall, though perhaps very gradually. Now, the flexprice commodities enter into the costs of the fixprice commodities; so when the prices of flexprice commodities are abnormally low, the prices of fixprice commodities should also fall, to

some extent. But if the low prices of the flexprice commodities are felt to be abnormal, and so probably temporary,
the tendency to reduce the prices of the fixprice commodities cannot be very strong. And so when the flexprice
prices recover—towards a normal level—the tendency to
raise the fixprice prices will not be very strong. The costs
which are reflected in fixprice prices are *normal* costs; and
in a slump, such as we have been discussing, normal costs
(which are a matter of judgement) will have fallen much
less than actual costs have fallen, since the fall in actual costs
is regarded as temporary.

All this makes good sense in terms of the old-style Trade
Cycle, even in terms of a major depression, such as that
which afflicted the world at the time when Keynes was
writing. The case for an expansion of effective demand,
however organized, as a means of mitigating the slump wins
hands down. When the surplus stocks have been reabsorbed,
the position becomes less clear. It may be granted that there
is no sharp line between conditions of surplus and conditions
of shortage; there is a zone, perhaps a fairly wide zone, in
which neither surplus nor shortage is acute. And there is a
corresponding zone in which the prices of flexprice commodities are neither abnormally low nor abnormally high.
Within that zone an expansion in demand may have no
more than a small effect, even on flexprice prices; for it is
when stocks are greatly in excess of normal that the costs of
carrying them become so oppressive. The carriage of more
or less normal stocks, such as will have been planned for
over a long period, should usually be relatively cheap. Thus

even when the acute phase of depression is passed, there may still be an opportunity for moderate 'engineered' expansion; it need not necessarily encounter an obstacle on the side of stocks. It does nevertheless appear, from what I have been saying, that there is always on this side a potential obstacle. It was not right to give the impression—the impression that one so easily gets from the *General Theory*—that the only obstacle to expansion, even to fast expansion, is scarcity of labour. There are other problems too.

The way in which this analysis can be carried over to the case of the open economy will by now be fairly obvious. We can see that there is an analogy between the distinction we have been making, between fixprice and flexprice behaviour (as applied to the closed economy), and the distinction between fixed and flexible exchanges. If a country is in the position (as many are) that it cannot much affect, by its own actions, the international prices that are important to it, a fixed rate of exchange keeps internationally traded goods fixprice goods, in nearly the same sense as we have been using that term.[8] So it is that the stocks which play the part we have been discussing are in that case, chiefly at least, stocks of foreign exchange. If, however, the exchange rate is allowed to float, with stocks of foreign exchange no longer being used as a stabilizer, the foreign goods as a whole become flexprice, not fixprice, goods. (The market for foreign exchange is then, *par excellence*, a speculative market.) Expansion may still be hampered by

[8] See p. 23 above.

scarcity of such commodities, scarcity which is revealed by a fall in the rate of exchange.

There is this effect, independently of any backwash on wages. I shall be coming to that in my third lecture.

II

MONEY, INTEREST AND LIQUIDITY

I pass to consider the other main parts of the Keynes theory
—the marginal efficiency of capital and the theory of money.
I shall take them together, for I think I can show that they
belong together. In the multiplier theory which I have been
discussing, Keynes is dealing with the effect of changes in
investment on income (and so on employment); he then
turns to examine the possibility of controlling investment
by monetary means. Both the marginal efficiency of capital
and the theory of money belong to this second subject.[1]

So much of his book is concerned with this second subject
that Keynes must have attached great importance to it; yet
for many of his followers its message has been purely nega-
tive. In the end (they conclude from what he says) there is
nothing important that can be done with monetary policy.
It can hardly be that Keynes took that view himself; he must
surely in some sense, perhaps a very weak sense, have been

[1] In my 'Mr. Keynes and the Classics', *Econometrica*, 1937, I similarly
reduced Keynes's three relations to two, taking the multiplier with the
marginal efficiency of capital to form the SI curve. I have come to feel
that the alternative grouping, which I am following here, is more revealing.

a monetarist. He has nevertheless been read to imply that there is nothing to be done with money. So all that remains, as an instrument of employment policy—or of *general* economic policy—is the government's budget. Thus it is that Keynesianism, in practice, has become fiscalism.

This is curious; as many have felt,[2] it needs to be explained. Now one of the things which needs to be noticed, if we are to have an explanation, is a thing which is embedded in the formal structure of his work. By taking the marginal efficiency of Capital as one topic, and the theory of money as another, he committed himself to the view that the link between money and investment is the rate of interest. He discusses (1) the effect of interest on investment, the marginal efficiency of capital, (2) the effect of money supply on interest, the liquidity preference theory of money. They are taken separately, because it is taken for granted that interest is the link.

But there is here an ambiguity. There are two distinct senses in which the term 'rate of interest' is used by economists. Sometimes it means a particular rate of interest, such as can be identified in practice on a particular market; sometimes it means something much vaguer, a kind of index of terms of lending, or of willingness to lend, quite generally. That interest, in this vaguer sense, is the link between money and investment is, I suppose, a fairly uncontroversial statement; I would certainly not dispute it myself. But this is not the sense in which *rate of interest* is

[2] See in particular the important book by Axel Leijonhufvud, *On Keynesian Economics and the Economics of Keynes*, 1968.

used in the *General Theory*. Keynes's rate of interest is a particular rate: the rate of interest at which a sound borrower, a borrower of unimpeachable credit, can raise a long-term loan on the market. Or, what is supposed to be much the same thing, the rate of interest on long-term government bonds.

Whether the rate of interest, in this latter sense, is an important determinant of investment is an empirical question; that is to say, it is a question which may be answered positively at some times and in some places, negatively in others. It is perfectly possible that in some countries and on some occasions it is to be answered positively; it was, however, the general impression, from discussions and investigations that took place soon after Keynes's ideas were first promulgated,[3] that in the England and in the America of the 1930s that was not the case. Businessmen did not appear to be greatly influenced by this 'rate of interest' in their investment decisions. That was a major reason why all this part of Keynes's book underwent an eclipse. It was a major reason why Keynesianism became fiscalism.

I am not inclined, myself, to jump to that conclusion; I believe that the monetary side of Keynes's teaching deserves much attention. It is nevertheless quite clear by this time— not only from the ancient evidence but from more recent experience which has seen so notable a decline in the practice

[3] The classic statement, so far as England is concerned, is the discussion of the results of a questionnaire to businessmen, that was published in the first number of *Oxford Economic Papers*, 1938.

of long-term borrowing—that it cannot be revived in just the form he gave it. It can only be revived in a form which lays less stress on the *long* rate of interest. Other aspects of the financial system—other rates of interest and other conditions of lending—must be kept in view as possible links. That is why it is desirable for the marginal efficiency of capital and the theory of money to be taken together.

Let us, however, begin by asking: why did Keynes lay such stress on the long rate of interest? So far as the *General Theory* is concerned, I think one can see the main answer. Though he often writes as if he is talking about the short-run position (or short-run equilibrium) of the economy— and that is the interpretation, or application, which his followers, with few exceptions, have had in mind—one can hardly overlook the presence of another interpretation. The 'unemployment equilibrium', of which he so often speaks, may be interpreted as a short-run equilibrium, a temporary situation; but there is clearly the suggestion that if something is not done about it, it will be long-lasting, perhaps permanent.[4] Stagnation, not depression! Now for dealing with a tendency to permanent unemployment, it is not just necessary that investment, now or this year, should be increased; what is required is that the whole level of investment should be raised, over a period of years. If monetary policy is to have this permanent effect, the whole gamut of interest rates (and terms of lending) must be

---

[4] The book was completed, it will be remembered, not in the depths of the depression, but during the upswing—the disappointing upswing— that began in 1934-5.

brought down and must stay down. Such a fall will imply a fall, a long-lasting fall, in the long rate of interest; and it may well be held that there can be no long-lasting fall in the long rate without a fall, also long-lasting, in the whole system of interest rates.

I believe that it is this interpretation which is most in line with the general course of Keynes's thinking in the *General Theory*; one of the things which it explains is the form that is taken by his theory of money. Why does he pay so much attention to his speculative motive for holding money? The market he so largely considers, in which the only choice that is open is a choice between holding money and holding bonds, is obviously a simplification. It is not a general description of a financial market; it is an isolation of the particular aspect of the financial market in which Keynes, for his particular purpose, was most interested. It was easy to show, granted this simplification, that occasions would arise when it would be (or would seem) more profitable to hold money than to hold bonds, in spite of the fact that the bonds carried a positive rate of interest, while the money carried none at all. It could happen if the interest on the bonds was expected to rise. For a rise in interest is equivalent to a fall in the price of bonds; an expected fall in price, in the near future, would cancel out the nominal yield. It is not the case, as often supposed, that this speculation implies that the operator is looking at the capital value of his portfolio, not at the income he is to derive from it. He will get a larger income, over any but the shortest period, if he is correct in his expectation, by postponing purchase.

Suppose that he expects the rate of interest on the bond to rise, from 4 to 5 per cent, within a year. £100 invested now will yield £4 per annum; if invested later, it looks like yielding £5 per annum; thus by delay there is a gain of £1 per annum, in perpetuity, against a loss of £4 (at the most) in the period of delay. Considered in income terms, this is quite a profitable investment. The 'barren' money, properly accounted for, is not without yield.

One can see, in the light of what has been said, why this speculation was so important to Keynes. His objective was to bring about a long-term fall in the long rate of interest; to such a policy bear speculation was a serious obstacle. The government might attempt to force up the price of long-term bonds; but so long as operators refused to believe in the higher price, they would sell, while they had (or could acquire) any bonds to sell, and wait for the price to come down. (How powerful such speculation can be was demonstrated practically, in England, soon after Keynes died. The Attlee government attempted to hold the long-term rate of government securities down to 3 per cent; but their patience was exhausted before that of the speculators.)

All this, however, is past history. A theory of money which is to apply more generally (especially one that is to apply in post-war inflationary conditions) can hardly be centred on the speculative motive in the way that seemed called for in 1936. It must indeed accept Keynes's major insight—that money is an asset, which can be weighed up against other assets in a balance-sheet, substituted for them or substituted by them. But it will not be sufficient to consider the substitution as simply a substitution between money and bonds. The balance-sheet must be considered much more generally.

We are indeed by now quite accustomed to considering it more generally. We have a well-established theory of the distribution of assets in a portfolio,[5] in which the speculation considered by Keynes appears as a special case. It is brought down from the central position it occupies in Keynes; it has a place nevertheless. But there are some things which are in Keynes which do not so easily survive; yet these also are things which need to be preserved. So we need something more than a portfolio selection theory; we need a theory of liquidity.

Liquidity (and so liquidity preference) does not appear in the portfolio selection theory, though bear speculation can easily be introduced. So they are something different. How this is I will try to explain.

The portfolio selection theory is concerned with choice under uncertainty. The regular method of dealing with choice under uncertainty is to make a separation between those things about which there is knowledge from those

[5] The theory has been stated in several ways, but from the present point of view they may be regarded as equivalent. Thus it is immaterial whether one considers the chooser to be maximizing some cardinal 'utility' (as is usual in the statements preferred by Tobin and other American economists) or whether one avoids that cardinal utility, as I personally prefer. See my paper on portfolio selection (*Critical Essays in Monetary Theory*, pp. 103-25). I should like to emphasize that this paper (and the present lecture) replace my old paper on Liquidity (*Economic Journal*, 1962), which was written at a time when my ideas on the subject were by no means fully formed.

things about which there is ignorance. The chooser is confronted with a number of 'states of the world'—or eventualities, as I would prefer to call them. He does not know which
eventuality will occur, but he does know what will be the
outcome of each choice that he may make, in each eventuality. Suppose that he has no more than a finite number of
alternatives from which to choose; and that there are no
more than a finite number of (relevant) eventualities. Then
the outcomes, of the various choices in the various
eventualities, can be arranged as a matrix—in which each
row shows the outcomes of one particular choice in the
various eventualities, while each column shows the outcomes of the various choices in one particular eventuality.
The chooser must make his choice between the rows, not
knowing which eventuality will occur.

Though he does not know which eventuality will occur,
he may be supposed to attach probabilities to them. Each
row will then have a probability distribution, which can
be described by moments in the usual statistical fashion.
Choice will depend on mean value (first moment) and on
higher moments (risk or uncertainty). According to his
willingness to bear risk, willingness to bear a greater risk in
order to get a higher return, he will choose one row or
another.

When the theory is set out in this way, it deals with a
single choice; and that is the point, I maintain, where
liquidity slips through. For liquidity is not a property of a
single choice; it is a matter of a sequence of choices, a related
sequence. It is concerned with the passage from the known

to the unknown—with the knowledge that if we wait we can have more knowledge. So it is not sufficient, in liquidity theory, to make a single dichotomy between the known and the unknown. There is a further category, of things which are unknown now, but will become known in time. These also must be fitted in.

One could fit them into the matrix, in the following way. Suppose that there are just two dates of decision—call them Christmas and Easter. We begin by representing the choice at Christmas in the usual way; the N columns of the matrix representing eventualities of which (on the knowledge available at Christmas) some *one* must occur, but it is not known which will occur. Then we suppose that as a result of what actually happens between Christmas and Easter, some of these eventualities get ruled out. For they have taken things to happen between Christmas and Easter which have not happened. So only n_1 of the original N eventualities survive at Easter. We suppose that it is known *at Christmas* that there will be this 'purge'; but it is not known which n_1 will survive. We can then classify the N Christmas eventualities into sub-sets, of $n_1, n_2 \ldots$ members, each sub-set containing the survivors of particular sequences of events between Christmas and Easter. By appropriate classification we can arrange it so that the sub-sets do not overlap.

We can then proceed to work on the rows in a similar manner. But now we must introduce a choice at Easter as well as a choice at Christmas; so a row of the matrix (now reinterpreted) must be made to represent a *double* choice. The double choices may, however, be reclassified as was done with the columns. The first m_1 rows represent the same Christmas choice with m_1 different Easter choices; the next m_2 another single Christmas choice with its associated Easter choices; and so on. We have thus partitioned our matrix, both by rows and by columns. Choice at Christmas is not between rows, but between sub-sets of rows, bands of rows; and events between Christmas and Easter make actual a particular sub-matrix, out of the sub-matrices of which the band is composed. Thus choice at

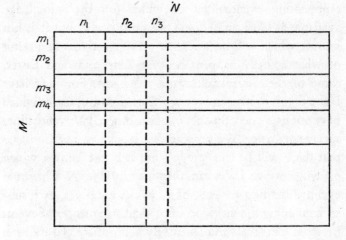

Christmas has been thrown into the same form as is used in the conventional statement, for the single choice without time-reference; but instead of choosing a single row, the constituents of which are single-valued outcomes, the chooser has now to select a band of rows, whose constituents are sub-matrices (as shown in the figure).

The important thing which is shown by this construction (which could easily be extended to a sequence of more than two choice-dates, with sub-matrices fitting into each other like Chinese boxes) is that there is an element in risk-bearing *over time* which escapes from the conventional presentation. For when the elements in the decision matrix cease to be single-valued outcomes, being transformed into sub-matrices, they develop a dimension which in the conventional presentation is suppressed. It becomes relevant to the 'Christmas' choice whether it carries with it a *wide* or a *narrow* band of 'Easter' alternatives—whether, that is to say, the choice admits of *flexibility*.

When the issue is stated in this very general manner, there is nothing particularly economic about it. Should Nelson, knowing that the French fleet has put to sea, keep his own fleet in a central position until his scouts have brought back more information, or should he follow his 'hunch' that it is going to Alexandria? Military questions, such as that, can readily be formulated in the same terms. But in military and suchlike applications there are so many kinds of flexibility; there is thus no ordering, no 'spectrum' from less flexible to more. In economics we are better placed.

For though there are many kinds of flexibility which are relevant to economic decisions, there is one that is outstanding. It is the flexibility that is given by the market. A firm which acquires a non-marketable asset—say a new factory, designed and equipped for its own particular purpose—has committed itself to a course of action, extending over a considerable time, with a fairly narrow band of subsequent choices attached to it. It has 'given hostages to fortune'. The acquisition of an easily marketable asset, on the other hand, can easily be revoked. There is not the same diminution of flexibility; the firm is in a position that is almost as flexible, after the acquisition, as before it. That, I suggest, is precisely what we mean by saying that the marketable asset possesses *liquidity*.

There are of course degrees of liquidity. As soon as we start thinking about a genuine balance-sheet, not just one that is artificially restricted to money and bonds, we are bound to recognize degrees of liquidity. Keynes did so himself. But there is only one place, so far as I know, where he gives a definition of degrees of liquidity. It is in the *Treatise*, not in the *General Theory*. He says that one asset is more liquid than another if it is 'more certainly realizable (*that is to say, convertible into money*) at short notice without loss'.[6] What exactly does this mean?

What kind of a loss—a loss compared to what? Not, surely, compared to what one had paid for it, the sort of loss which will be 'recorded in the books'? Economic decisions are forward-looking; what must be compared are things which may happen in the future. It is common experience, on an imperfect market, that the price which can be got from a quick sale is less than that which could be got with time and trouble; the buyer who will give the best price takes some finding. Sale 'at short notice' must then involve a 'loss', in comparison with what could be got with

[6] *Treatise*, Vol. II, p. 67.

longer notice. That is one of the things which is implied in Keynes's definition; but we should surely agree that things which can only be sold on such an imperfect market must be imperfectly liquid; they can have no more than a low degree of liquidity.

If an asset is to be liquid, in a narrower sense, it must be tradeable on a regular market; it must at all times have a regular market price. But such a price may be very variable, or fairly stable. What Keynes is saying is that if the price is very variable, the asset is still imperfectly liquid—because of the risk that at a date chosen at random (and the date of disposal, it must be emphasized, is uncertain) the price at which the asset can be sold will be *abnormally* low. For if that were to happen, he would have *chanced* to find himself in the same position as he would have occupied if he had acquired a less marketable asset—the price which could be got from a quick sale would be less than what could be got by waiting. In the case of the less marketable asset, it is certain that there will be such a loss; in the case of the marketable but price-unstable asset the loss is no more than possible. But the risk of loss remains.

Such assets are unsatisfactory, as sources of liquidity, because of the risk that a moment will come for switching to some other asset, a switch which would be profitable if the asset that is held had retained its value, but which is rendered unprofitable by the fact that the value is temporarily depressed. So by holding the imperfectly liquid asset the holder has narrowed the band of opportunities which may be open to him; this is just to choose a narrower band, in the sense of our previous analysis. As the market jargon goes, he has 'locked himself in'.

It follows from this discussion of the nature of liquidity that the principles of choice, when liquidity is important, are substantially different from those that are taken into account in the conventional theory of portfolio selection. There are in fact just two cases in which that theory applies exactly—cases in which there is no question of liquidity, properly understood.

One is the case in which choice has to be made once and for all—when it is known that there will be no subsequent opportunity for changing one's mind. The optimum port-folio should then be selected purely on the principle of spreading risks. (It should be noticed that if the theory is interpreted in this sense, there is no opportunity for specu-lation, and hence for a speculative motive for holding money. Investment is purely for 'income'; so long as there is any security which promises a positive income, no money will be held.)

The other, a more interesting case, is that in which there are sequential choices, but the sequential choices are *inde-pendent*. Choice at 'Easter' will be just as wide whatever choice is made at 'Christmas'. This will happen if the choice made at Christmas can be costlessly undone. If there are no costs of investment and disinvestment, it is only necessary for the investor to look to the immediate future, and so to maximize the expected 'utility' of his portfolio at 'Easter' or at the next point at which a decision is to be taken. No actual investor is ever in that position, but some professional

financiers may sometimes be nearly in that position. To
them portfolio selection theory will apply exactly; and the
Keynesian analysis of the speculative motive will also apply.
There is no reason why they should not hold money for a
speculative motive; if they have bearish expectations it may
pay them to do so.

Nevertheless, when one is thinking of a professional
financier, to suppose that he has no alternative but to hold
money *or* bonds is hardly useful. We should surely give him
a wider choice. Then, even if he is bearish, he should be
able to find some short-dated security, on which the maxi-
mum capital loss, in the near future, is so small that it must
be outweighed by the interest earned. Then, when he is
bearish, he will switch, not into money, but into bills. So
what will be affected by his bearishness is not the 'rate of
interest' (in the sense of marginal rate of substitution between
bonds and money) but the spread between short and long
rates (in the sense of marginal rate of substitution between
bonds and bills).

Much has been written, since Keynes, on that spread—or
on the term structure of interest rates more broadly considered.[7] We have had an 'expectations theory',[8] which is
in effect an analysis of how the term structure would work,
in a perfect market, such that costs of investment and disinvestment could be disregarded. This theory has been
tested against the facts; and it has usually been found that

[7] There is a useful summary of the literature in R. S. Masera, *The Term
Structure of Interest Rates*.
[8] Such as that which I produced myself in *Value and Capital*, Chapter 13.

it does not fit the facts very well. One must conclude that even this market, this purely financial market, is not in most countries a perfect market, in the required sense. There are costs of investment which are sufficient to matter. It follows, from what has been said, that even those who operate upon such markets must pay some attention to liquidity.

Even those whose costs of disinvestment are small will have to do so; even the professional financier will have to do so; so there will be some spread, in his balance-sheet, between more and less liquid assets. Yet his least liquid assets, as compared with most of the assets that are held outside the financial sector, are quite liquid. Does not this suggest that it is outside the financial sector, or to the boundaries of the financial sector, that we should be looking, for the major effects of liquidity—or illiquidity?

Consider the case of a manufacturing business; and proceed, as before, by looking at its balance-sheet. Most of its assets will be physical (or real) assets: land and buildings, plant and machinery, stocks and work in progress (the conventional accountant's classification). There will also be financial assets (and liabilities): cash in hand and at the bank, debts arising in the course of trading, and (perhaps) some reserves. The nominal 'debt' which is due to its shareholders need not be considered. These assets may, however, be cross-classified in what for our present purpose is a more meaningful way. First, there are assets which are required for the normal running of the business; I call these *running assets*. Secondly, there are assets which are not normally used, but are kept because they *may* be wanted. I call these (in a more general sense) *reserve assets*.[9]

The line between running and reserve, so defined, is not the same as that between physical and financial. Most of the running assets, indeed, will be physical assets. Work in progress is the perfect example of a running asset; but most of the plant and machinery will also reckon as running assets. It is nevertheless not uncommon for some machines to be held as reserves; they are not normally used, but are kept as a fall-back in the case of a breakdown or of some other emergency. Stocks of materials may obviously be held as reserves in a similar way. Thus there are both physical running assets and physical reserve assets.

Cash in hand, on this classification, will evidently reckon as a financial running asset. So will the debts due from customers; while the debts owed by the firm (the other side of trade credit) will appear as running liabilities.

Every asset is held for its yield; if it was not profitable to hold it, it would not be an asset. The profit that is derived from its running assets will usually be the main part of the profit of the business; but it is generally true that the yield on a particular running asset is by no means easy to identify. Withdraw some particular machine, or some particular half-finished product, and you stop the whole process of which it is a part. Thus the running assets of the firm are a bundle of complements; the bundle as a whole has a yield but it cannot, in general, be imputed to the separate items.

[9] This is the same distinction as I made in the *Two Triads* (*Critical Essays,* esp. pp. 38 ff.).

The same applies to the financial running assets. The money balance, held by the firm, is one of the bundle of complements. It is true that the money balance will not be constant; even a firm which is in a stationary position, neither expanding nor contracting, will not have a stationary money balance. Its cash will fluctuate, perhaps weekly, perhaps seasonally, perhaps on some other pattern. But when averaged over time—usually not a very long time— it will come out, for a stationary firm in conditions of steady prices, fairly constant. It needs that balance, on the average, for normal running. The dates of payment for inputs and receipt from outputs do not match exactly; it needs a money balance to ensure that it can pay for inputs, at the date when payment is due.

The money balance that is held as a running asset is the same as that held for Keynes's 'transactions motive'; it is our particular firm's contribution to the 'transactions demand for money'. It is because of the complementarity between running assets that the proportionality, so commonly assumed, between the transactions demand for money and the total money value of output has been found to be plausible. It is nevertheless unwise to push it far. In the short run, with *given* monetary arrangements, and with a constant rate of expansion of the money value of output,[10]

[10] That there may well be a special requirement for money balances (or other financial inputs) during a process of expansion—when there are poor opportunities for borrowing, so that investment must be financed out of gradually accumulated savings—is a point that was familiar to many of the older economists. Its contemporary relevance to the problems of less-developed countries has been stressed in a recent book by Ronald McKinnon (*Money and Capital in Economic Development*, Brookings, 1973).

some constancy in the ratio may indeed be expected; but this gives no reason to expect that there will be constancy over a longer period. For as soon as we accept that the business demand for money (which must usually be a large part of total transactions demand) is of the nature of an input into the productive process (a 'stock input' like land) we shall expect to find that in the longer run (with 'technical change') the input coefficient may be varied. Methods will be sought for, and will be discovered, by which the use of this input can be economized; if rates of interest are high (so that the opportunity cost of the money input is high), there will be a stimulus to the discovery of such methods— 'induced invention'.[11] But we should not conclude, from this pressure for economizing, that a secular decline in the input coefficient is to be expected; for methods which improve the *productivity* of money holding may also be discovered, and surely have been discovered. It is much safer to hold money in a bank (provided that it is a safe bank) than to hold it in cash; that is one way in which the *productivity* of holding money, if properly reckoned, can be increased. Reductions in the cost of making transactions— as again by the use of bank credit rather than cash—may work the same way.[12]

[11] The discussion of 'induced inventions' in my *Capital and Time* (1973), pp. 120–2, exactly applies.

[12] It is surely much more reasonable, when one is concerned with secular changes in the demand for money, to look for the effects of such technical changes than to postulate an 'income-elasticity' in the manner of Friedman. Such a postulate explains nothing; on the other line what has happened could be explained.

We are left with the financial assets held as reserves—for liquidity. We should expect to find that these will be important; yet we will often find, on examination of actual balance-sheets, that there appear to be no such assets. Yet the firm, which appears to have no liquid assets, is not illiquid. It has a substitute for liquid assets in the form of assured borrowing power, usually from a bank. The borrowing power may be contractual, in the form of an agreed overdraft; but it need not be contractual. If the firm knows that it can get funds when it needs them, it need keep no liquid assets as reserves.

Firms of different kinds will have different needs for flexibility, and hence for liquidity; but when this is allowed for, we should surely expect that the larger a firm is, the larger will be its requirement for liquid funds, either in its own possession or securely available. In a country where banks are large, the liquidity requirement of a small firm is a small matter to the bank; thus if the firm enjoys good credit, its liquidity requirements can readily be met by bank borrowing. Larger firms (we should nevertheless expect) would be unable to get from banks all that they require; so they would have to keep, or to try to keep, some liquid assets of their own.

Much depends, in this matter, on legal arrangements; it would nevertheless seem helpful, fairly generally, to think of business (we can now include financial business) as divided into two sectors—one which mainly relies for its liquidity on the actual possession of liquid assets, and one which is mainly supported by assured (or apparently assured) borrowing power. Let us call them *auto-sector* and *overdraft sector* respectively (remembering, however, that the financing of the overdraft sector need not take the form of formal overdrafts). There will be some countries—such, I suppose, as the U.S.—where the auto-sector is large and the overdraft sector small; in others, such as the U.K., the overdraft sector is much larger.

The pure auto-economy (with no overdraft sector) has been much studied by monetary theorists; the working of monetary policy in such an economy is by now fairly well understood.[13] The financial markets (at least) are supposed to behave as flexprice markets; so when the monetary authority increases the supply of money by buying securities —that is the only way in which on its own initiative it can increase the supply of money—it will tend to raise the price of those securities and thence, by a process of substitution along a chain of substitutes, it will raise the price-level of securities (above what it would have been) quite generally. We may express this by saying that it lowers the 'rate of interest'—not the long rate in particular, but the rate of interest in the more general sense. This has two effects which it is most important to distinguish.

The first is that which seems mainly to have been in the mind of Keynes himself. A reduction in the 'rate of interest' stimulates investment—because there are marginal projects which would not have been profitable at the higher, but are profitable at the lower, rate (the marginal efficiency of

[13] Thanks, of course, in large measure to Keynes; but to the Keynes of the *Treatise* at least as much as to the Keynes of the *General Theory*.

capital). There is no reason to doubt the reality of this effect, considered as a long-term phenomenon; but even when 'rate of interest' is interpreted more widely than Keynes was usually in the habit of doing, there remains some doubt about its short-run importance.

In the light of our present discussion we can see why. When a firm undertakes real investment, it acquires a non-liquid asset; but it loses a liquid asset (or incurs a corresponding liability) on the other side. In either case, its liquidity is diminished. Now if (initially) its liquidity was satisfactory, or more than satisfactory, this may not much matter. But from a position in which there are widespread doubts about liquidity—and it is from such a position that an expansionary monetary policy will most usually seem to be called for—a mere reduction in 'rate of interest' will not give much stimulus to investment.

Relief may nevertheless come from a second effect. The rise in the prices of securities increases the value of reserves (provided that not all reserves are kept in money form)—thus increasing liquidity. Some increase in real investment should therefore be possible without diminishing liquidity, relatively to what it would have been if the fall in interest had not occurred.

It is however necessary, if this relief is to be substantial, that the reserves should be held in a form which is sensitive to interest changes. Reserves that are held in 'shorts' can hardly be significantly sensitive. A portfolio of bills, of one-year maturity, accruing at various dates within the year, will change in value by less than 1 per cent when the rate of interest changes by 1 per cent; rarely enough to be significant. If reserves are held in 'longs' (or in equities) the effect may, on occasion, be much more substantial; but here we are back at Keynes's old dilemma—that it is hard for monetary policy to affect the long rate of interest very much, because of speculation. It would yet appear that too ample a supply of short-dated securities (near-money) must make it more difficult to exercise monetary policy, because of the obstacle which it puts in the way of a substantial liquidity effect.

Most of this can be put into reverse for the case of a monetary policy which is leaning the other way. The principal way in which monetary policy can diminish investment (to prevent 'over-heating') is by diminishing liquidity. That is more easily done (in an auto-economy) if the reserves of businesses have to be held in not too liquid a form. But here again the Keynesian analysis of the speculative motive is relevant. The effect on the prices of securities (and hence on liquidity) will be much greater if the monetary authority looks as if it 'means business'—so that pressure will be maintained, if necessary, until it takes effect—than if it seems to be fearful of the effects of its operations, so that the market feels that at any moment they may be reversed.

All this assumes a pure auto-economy. Almost every (non-socialist) actual economy has an auto-sector; most, however, have an overdraft sector (in the broad sense we have given the term) as well. It will thus be useful, for the sake of contrast, to consider the working of monetary policy in a pure overdraft economy.

In a pure overdraft economy where firms kept no liquid reserves, they would be wholly dependent, for their liquidity, on the banks. The liquidity of business would be directly controllable by the banks. It is conceivable, however, that there might be no control save through interest. A firm would know that it could call on its banker for unlimited funds at the announced rate of interest; so it would be in the 'regular' Keynesian position—any project which looked like yielding that rate of interest (with allowance for risk) would be undertaken, and not otherwise. A particular firm which works on overdraft may indeed be in that position with respect to any investment it feels inclined to undertake; but there is clearly no need that that should be the general position. It is more reasonable, in general, to suppose that the firm's capacity to borrow depends upon its credit; the liquidity of the firm will then depend upon the extent of the funds which it thinks itself (and is thought by those who trade with it) to be able to borrow.

Such a firm will be more liquid if it has an agreed overdraft—a contractual right to borrow, up to a limit—than it would be if it had no contractual right, only an informal understanding. But this is only an example of the ways in which it is possible, in an overdraft economy, for banks to affect investment by varying liquidity, more powerfully, it may well be, than by varying interest charges. There are many ways open; even a speech by a banker may affect the liquidity of potential borrowers.

What, however, of the liquidity of the banks themselves? Banks, surely, have liquid reserves of their own; so that, at least at first sight, they may be thought to constitute an auto-sector—even though all outside the banking system are organized on overdraft lines. Historically, no doubt, the banks have begun as an auto-sector; the individual bank controlled its own reserves, and had to look to its own liquidity, just like a non-banking firm in an auto-economy. It is easy for a theorist, even now, to suppose that that is the way the banking system works—that monetary policy is exercised by changes in liquidity pressure, by central banks on 'member banks'. Actuality, by now, is surely in most cases very different. Central banks and member banks do not deal with each other 'at arm's length'; they have many means of communication which do not depend on market signals, such as rates of interest. The closer knit the banking system becomes, the closer the relation of members to central bank approaches the overdraft form. The members are independent upon the centre, in much the same way as the firm which relies on overdrafts depends upon its bank. This is concealed in the way that accounts are presented; but more and more it represents the reality.[14]

It would seem from this analysis—very tentative analysis,

[14] When we turn to the international banking system, of which the Central Banks of different countries are member banks, while the IMF is no more than an embryo central bank (rather like the Bank of England in much of its early history), we find the same apparent auto-relations, mixed up with strong tendencies to mutual dependence. They begin from the gold exchange standard, and lead—who knows where? I have here been following Keynes (of the *General Theory*) in confining attention to the working of a closed system, averting my eyes from the international scene. I have nevertheless no doubt that the latter could be discussed, and could usefully be discussed, along the lines which I have been trying to sketch out.

for I have been venturing in these last paragraphs into what for economists is still a largely uncharted field—that the relative impotence of monetary policy (the lesson that fiscal-ists have so largely drawn from Keynes) is not a universal characteristic; it is a characteristic of an auto-economy. In an overdraft economy (or in an economy with a large over-draft sector) the banking system is much more powerful. The power is nevertheless one that has to be used with discretion. For its existence depends upon a conviction in business that banks are dependable. If that conviction is lost, there is bound to be a swing back to the holding of owned reserves, which will then appear to be more dependable. So there will be a swing back to the auto-economy.

That is one danger; but there is another, which in these days is more pressing. I have assumed, in the foregoing, that money, and securities with values that are fairly reliable in terms of money, *are* liquid assets. But why is money liquid? Because it can be used to buy things—things that *may* be required. When prices, in general, are fairly stable, there is no doubt that money possesses that attribute; that it serves, pre-eminently, as a store of value. In prolonged inflation, that attribute is weakened. It is only in hyper-inflation that it is lost altogether; so that money, and money-substitutes, cease to offer the *freedom* which their possession normally conveys. We have not, in any of the countries which are experiencing the current inflation (save perhaps in a few the economies of which are not sophisticated), come near to reaching that point; but it could be reached. It is no more than discernible upon the horizon; but it is discernible. The time has already come when we need to bring ourselves to think rationally about it.

I have come to feel that one of the worst things about Keynes's doctrine—or rather, perhaps, of the way he put his doctrine—is the impression he gives that Liquidity Preference is wholly, and always, bad. One sees how it came about, when one considers the time when he was writing; it was right at that time, but it is far from being always right. Excess of liquidity preference is indeed bad; there is no doubt about that. But hyper-inflation, in which there is no liquid asset, and hence no opportunity for liquidity preference, is also bad; though Keynes no doubt took this for granted, his theory does not make it clear enough. The trouble lies deep in his version of short-run macroeconomics, in which one form of investment appears as good as another. Only investment expenditure is taken into account; the productivity of the investment is neglected. (One remembers those pyramids!) Once one accepts that one form of investment is not as good as another, it follows that it is socially productive that the form of investment should be wisely chosen. It cannot be wisely chosen if it is too much hurried. The social function of liquidity is that it gives time to think.

III

WAGES AND INFLATION

It is time—you will probably be thinking it is quite time—
to turn to wages. It is by the upset with which it has been
associated in the field of wages that Keynesianism in practice
has most grievously disappointed the hopes which it had
aroused; much of what I have been saying may well seem
to be of small importance, compared to that. 'Wage-
inflation'; it is with us all, as an immediately pressing problem. That it is closely connected with Keynesian economics
—that it is a problem of Keynesian economics—can hardly
be denied. So I cannot conclude without some attention to
what Keynes said about wages; and without some effort to
decide just what, in the light of our own experience, we
should now think ought to have been said.

One of the things in the *General Theory* which caused
most trouble to its first readers (I speak from experience)
was the habit of working in what were called 'wage-units'.
Income in wage-units; even money supply in wage-units;
they seemed at first sight very awkward concepts. They
depended (we learned at last) upon a principle, very important to Keynes, which I shall call the *wage-theorem*. When
there is a general (proportional) rise in money wages, says

the theorem, the *normal* effect is that all prices rise in the same proportion—provided that the money supply is increased in the same proportion (whence the rate of interest will be unchanged). It is not maintained that the wage-theorem will be true in all conditions; some of the conditions for its validity will concern us later. But Keynes clearly thought that it was usually true. It is because of the theorem that investment, and income, and money supply are measured in wage-units; for it follows from the theorem that when so measured, they are *independent* of the level of money wages.

All expositors of Keynes (including myself) have found this procedure a difficulty. The wage-theorem could not be understood until one had grasped the rest of the theory; yet the rest of the theory (when expounded in the way Keynes expounded it) could not be understood without the wage-theorem. We had to find some way of breaking the circle. The obvious way of doing so was to begin by setting out the rest (multiplier, liquidity preference and so on) on the assumption of *fixed* money wages. Then, with that behind one, it was fairly easy to go on to the wage-theorem. That is what we did—I still think that it was what we had to do —but the consequences of doing it were serious.

For when the Keynes theory is set out in this text-book manner (as I shall call it) it is bound to give the impression that there are just two 'states' of the economy: a 'state of unemployment' in which money wages are constant, and a 'state of full employment' in which pressure of demand causes wages to rise. So 'full employment' is an 'inflation barrier'. As long as employment is less than full, even if it is only marginally less than full, there should be no wage-inflation. So all we need do, in order to have 'full employment without inflation', is suitably to control demand.

Though this text-book version is a view that has come out of Keynes's economics, it is by no means clear that it was Keynes's own. It is hard to see that in his book he has *any* theory about the causation of changes in money wages. He did indeed distinguish between the state of full employment in which wages rise because of labour scarcity—as a consequence, therefore, of things which he had taken into account—and the state of unemployment, in which there is no reason for wages to rise *from that cause*. He must have known, from experience, that wages did sometimes fall in a state of high unemployment; but he did not concern himself with such falls except to point out that by the wage-theorem they should have no *real* effect. The same should presumably hold, in a state of unemployment, for *rises* in money wages. Thus the view which emerges from the *General Theory* is more radical than 'full employment without inflation'; it is nothing less than the view that inflation does not matter.

I do not suppose that Keynes held, at all consistently, to this radical view; in later writings, written during the war, he seems to have moved much nearer to the 'full employment without inflation' position. The extreme position which he takes, by implication, in the *General Theory*, is surely to be explained by the circumstances of its time. Inflation, in 1936, seemed far from being a danger; the important thing to say was that deflation would not help. That is the practical thing that Keynes was saying. It was right, then; but it was not the whole story. To have made it into a general principle, working both ways, was surely (we must now say) very unfortunate.

We cannot manage, nowadays, without some theory (or at least some view) about changes in money wages. There seem to be three alternatives.

One, the most popular, is also the nearest to that which I have ascribed to Keynes (the Keynes of 1936). 'Wage-push' is distinguished from 'demand-pull', as now it has to be; but the causes of 'wage-push', on this view, are exogenous, even non-economic. They are matters of trade union organization, of politics, or of public opinion. So if we dislike the effects of the wage-push, we must deal with it directly—by negotiation between government and unions, by political pressure or by legal freezes. We should indeed see, by a suitable fiscal policy, that demand-pull inflation is not added to the wage-push; but that is as far as we should go. The Keynesian independence between wage-policy and other economic policy is by this school still maintained.

A second alternative, which also descends from some Keynesian ideas, leads to opposite conclusions. It begins from the observation—itself (surely) quite noncontroversial —that the text-book opposition between the two states, of unemployment and of full employment, is too sharp. Something has been overlooked; the obvious fact of the specialization of labour. Particular labour scarcities are bound to be revealed, in a process of expansion, while there

Tobin?

is still, in total, considerable unemployment. Thus wages will start rising much before 'full employment'. The rise is ascribed, as in the text-book version of Keynes, to demand-pull; but it begins to appear while there is still unemployment.

There should thus, on this second view, be a band, supposedly a wide band, in which there is a relation between the rate of wage-rise and the rate of unemployment. The lower the unemployment, the higher the rate of wage-rise. This is the relation which is supposed to be detected in the well-known 'Phillips curve'—the 'trade-off' between unemployment and inflation.

The Phillips curve, as originally presented, was a statistical relation, a relation to which certain figures appeared to conform. But a pure statistical relation must be judged accidental, unless there is some reason behind it; the obvious way of making sense of Phillips's relation is that which I have just explained. So if we call that the 'Phillips theory' it may not be inappropriate. The Phillips theory, then, is a pure 'demand-pull' theory; we may grant that if demand-pull is the only factor at work, something like the Phillips behaviour is intelligible. But it leaves wage-push quite out of account.

I do not believe that it can be left out of account; nor, however, that it should be treated as exogenous. I believe that it has, at least to some extent, economic causes, and that these causes are important. So I come to the third alternative, which is that which (as you will suppose) I prefer.

I need, in order to explain it, a little preparation. We

must look, a little more closely than economists often do, at the nature of the labour market.

There is a distinction which I made, long ago, in my 1932 book on *Wages* from which I may begin.[1] (There is much in that book which I would now reject, but this I think still stands.) It is the distinction between casual employment, the single job implying no durable relationship, and regular employment, in which people work together and go on working together. There is a similar distinction in other markets; but while most (though not all) of the markets for goods are casual—the shopper is not tied to a particular shop, nor does his purchase imply commitment to further purchases—most labour markets, and all the more important labour markets, are regular. Now it is necessary, purely on grounds of efficiency, in regular employment, that both parties, employer and employed, should be able to look forward to some durability in their relationship. Yet if the worker is to be free to move (and if he is not free to move it is semi-slavery) there can be no such reliability unless there is contentment, or at least some degree of contentment. So it is necessary for efficiency that the wage-contract should be felt, by both parties but especially by the worker, to be *fair*.

But what is fairness? Economists have endeavoured to give definitions, sophisticated definitions; but I doubt if they are much to the point. What is needed is not that some third party, or arbitrator, applying general principles, should prescribe a fair wage; what is needed is that the worker

[1] *Theory of Wages*, 1932 or 1963, pp. 60 ff.

himself should feel that he is being treated fairly. In fairness, in that sense, there are many elements; and they do not fit together at all well. It is unfair, says A, that B (whom I think is no more deserving than I am) should get a higher wage than I do; but B, who gets the higher wage, may also think it unfair if A's wage is rising faster than his. C feels it to be unfair if his employer is making large profits, but does not raise his wages; but if he does raise C's wages, others (whose employers are not making such large profits) will think it unfair. It is felt to be unfair if prices are rising and wages are not rising in the same proportion; but it is also felt to be unfair if wages are rising faster than prices, but not so much faster as they did a year or two ago. And so on, and so on. A system of wages which will satisfy all the demands for fairness that may be made upon it is quite unattainable. No system of wages, when it is called in question, will ever be found to be fair.

That has always been true; how is it then that we have got on, in the past, as well as we have? Only because the wage-system has not much been called in question. That can happen; but it is necessary, for it to happen, that the system of wages should be well established, so that it has the sanction of custom. It then becomes what is expected; and (admittedly on a low level of fairness) what is expected is fair.

It was commonly observed, in the old days before the 'Keynesian revolution', that wages were *sticky*. Sometimes this meant no more than that the labour market behaved in the way which I have attributed to fixprice markets; wages did not necessarily fall when there was unemployment, nor necessarily rise when there was shortage of labour. But fix-price behaviour, in the labour market, must surely be different from that which I formerly discussed. It cannot be associated with stock-holding; for labour, as one of the older economists put it, is 'as perishable as cut flowers'. There must be a different explanation; it is to be found, I would suggest, in those characteristics of the labour market which I have just been describing. Employers were reluctant to raise wages, simply because of labour scarcity; for to offer higher wages to particular grades of labour that had become scarce would upset established differentials. They were reluctant to cut wages, simply because of unemployment; for if they did so they would alienate those whom they continued to employ. The 'stickiness' is not a matter of 'money illusion'; it is a matter of continuity. It would of course be reinforced by the *standard rates* of trade union-ism; but there would be a tendency in the same direction, even apart from trade union pressure.

Just how much weight should be given to such considerations will vary, of course, from country to country; and will vary with the stage of industrialization, or semi-industrialization, that has been reached. I am influenced by what I know of British wage-history; I do not know how far British experience is typical. May I, however, take the British case as an example? It will help to explain what I mean; and it is surely relevant when one is talking about Keynes.

There is no doubt that before 1914, and again in the inter-

war period, British wages were decidedly sticky; though
the indexes of wages most generally available, being averages
of many industries, do not fully reveal how sticky wages
were. The best index we have (it is not very reliable)[2] shows
a fall in the 'average money wage' by about 5 per cent from
1900 to 1904, and then a rise to about 5 per cent *above 1900*
by 1913. But closer examination shows that a large part of
this fluctuation was concentrated on a few particular trades,
that were known to be 'cycle-sensitive'. Wages in these
trades varied very widely, and were expected to vary,
between times of good and bad trade. (The fact that in some
of these trades—coal and steel—there were, or had been,
selling-price sliding scales, by which wages varied with the
price of the product, must surely be taken as an indication
that wages were responding, not to employment, but to
profits.) In other trades, in the majority of occupations, the
movement of wages must have been very slow indeed.

Then came the war—World War I. By 1920 the wage-
index (with 1914 = 100) had risen to 280; but by 1923 it
had fallen from that to 194. A drop of nearly one-third,
and no social revolution! And subsequently, very remark-
ably, the stickiness was resumed.

There was a further fall in the worst years of the great
depression; but even in 1933 the wage-index had fallen no
more than 5 per cent below its level in the mid-twenties, a
level which by 1937 had again been reached. The fall from
1926 to 1933 was no greater than the fall from 1900 to 1904;
but the slump was far greater! All things allowed for, we

[2] Mitchell and Deane, *British Historical Statistics*, 1962, pp. 342–5.

may surely say that in the inter-war years the stickiness which had marked the wage-system before 1914 simply reappeared.

The contrast between 1920–3 and 1930–3 is indeed very striking. Unemployment was far greater in the later depression than in the earlier, but the fall in wages was far less. So the difference just cannot be explained in the Phillips manner, in terms of unemployment. There must be something else.

One can clearly go some way towards explaining the acceptance, without revolution, of the enormous wage-cuts of 1920–3 by observing that prices were falling just as fast.[3] Thus there was no cut in real wages (on the average). But this does not explain the difference in behaviour, for in 1930–3 also prices were falling; they were falling so fast that the real wage, of those who stayed in employment, actually rose. One cannot altogether explain what happened by working in terms of real wages, though it helps.

The essential difference, surely, between the two cases is that the cuts of 1921–3 came after a rise, a very rapid rise; while the cuts of 1930–3 came after a phase when the wage-level had been stabilized, or in the case of some industries was already sagging. The principal reason why wages came down so easily in the earlier case was that the rise in 1920 had been so fast that it was not believed in. The wages paid in 1923 were lower in money terms but not in real terms; they were, however, being paid in a more reliable, and

[3] A. C. Pigou, *Aspects of British Economic History, 1918–25*, 1947, pp. 230–1.

therefore more acceptable, money. Wages were fluid in 1919–21 because confidence in money was impaired; when that confidence was restored, they became sticky again.

I am sorry to inflict on you all this background; but it is background to Keynes. At the time when he was writing, wages (at least in Britain) were sticky; it was of course a consequence of that stickiness that what I have called the text-book version of Keynes was accepted as easily as it was. But later, in the fifties and sixties, while Keynesian economics has been put into practice, wages have not been sticky; why?

The second world war, like the first, upset the wage-structure. After the first, as we have seen, the stickiness was resumed, but after the second it was not. One of the reasons, it can hardly be doubted, was that the second upset lasted longer; it was not until 1952, after the Korean war, that an opportunity occurred, such as had occurred in 1920, six years after 1914. That in itself made resumption more difficult. The principal reason, however, was a change in priorities. The 1920s had set a high value on stability—price-stability and wage-stability—and had paid far too little attention to the maintenance of employment. There was bound to be a reaction; and in that reaction the Keynes theory played a part. So the fifties made the maintenance of employment an over-riding priority (not that they always succeeded, but this was the intention); stability, in contrast, seemed a secondary matter. And there is no doubt that for a time the new system seemed to work. It met, in time, its own troubles; but they took time to appear.

Thus there are two stages, in the history of the last twenty years, which have to be distinguished. It is not easy to put dates upon them, for the passage from stage I to stage II was often gradual; and in some countries it began sooner, in some later. All one can say is that by the late sixties there had been a fairly general movement into stage II.

I will try to describe the two stages, in rather general terms.

Stage I inflation is demand inflation; it works, in the main, on Phillips lines. Private investment continues to fluctuate in its old 'cyclical' manner; for the *real* causes of the old trade cycle (which I need not discuss, for they are written in the text-books) have not been removed. But there is superimposed upon the old cycle a 'Keynesian' fiscal and monetary policy which (we shall not now be surprised to discover) is more successful in raising the general level of activity, over the cycle as a whole, than in damping down fluctuations. Thus there is less unemployment, in the slump, than there was in the old days; but in the boom there is more inflation.

As in the old days, the wages that rise in the boom are wages in particular industries—the cycle-sensitive industries which are still with us. But in the old days those wages, which rose in the boom, fell in the slump; now they rise in the boom but in the (moderated) slump they do not fall. They therefore unsettle wages in other industries. There was always of course some unsettlement, due to movement of labour from non-expanding to expanding industries; so if a boom, even in the old days, lasted long enough, the rise in wages, which began in cycle-sensitive industries, would to some extent be generalized. In spite of the specialization of labour, labour scarcity would spread. But what happens in the new conditions is more than that. Wages rise, in the non-expanding industries, not because of labour scarcity, but because of *unfairness*; because the workers in the non-expanding industries feel that they are getting left behind. This did not happen, to anything like the same extent, in the old days; for the high wages that were paid in the boom, in the cycle-sensitive industries, were regarded as temporary. It did not seem so unfair to the workers in other industries that they should be paid, during the boom, relatively low wages; for they could be sure that the time would come when they would benefit from their stability. But in the new conditions, when the high wages, induced by boom scarcities, come to seem more permanent, there is far more pressure, from the workers in other industries, for their wages to 'catch up'. The pressure may take the form of strikes, but that may not be necessary. Any arbitrator will agree that a rise in wages is 'fair'. And it will be clear to employers that they must raise wages for the sake of 'good industrial relations'.

I would allow for the beginnings of this process in stage I; the characteristic of stage II is that this 'social' pressure for rising wages has become dominant. It is no longer the case that the main force that is raising wages is labour scarcity. Wages rise, whether or not there is labour scarcity; so they rise in slumps as much, or nearly as much, as in booms. Everyone, on some comparison or other, feels left behind. The electricians get a rise, so the gasmen must follow; but when the gasmen get their rise, it is the electricians who feel themselves to be treated unfairly. In terms of just two industries, the behaviour sounds exaggerated; but generalize it over many, and is it not what happens? Is not this the inflation, which is perfectly consistent with trade depression, the 'stagnation-inflation' which was so widely experienced in 1970-1?

It will be useful, in order to understand this condition more deeply, to go back to the wage-theorem, considering it a little further, first of all in theoretical terms.

As the wage-theorem is often stated, it is no more than a piece of comparative statics. We start from an 'equilibrium' at a particular level of money wages. We then observe that the system could also be in equilibrium at a higher level of money wages, with prices adjusted in the same proportion as the wage-level has risen, and a money supply adjusted to the extent that is needed to finance the higher *value* of output. The value of output, in money terms, would be raised; but real wages, and indeed all *real* price-ratios, would be unchanged. When so stated, as a piece of comparative statics, the wage-theorem is identical with an extreme form of the quantity theory of money; for on the quantity theory a change in money supply affects no *real* price-ratios, wages and prices being again adjusted in the same proportion. So long as we stick to comparative statics, to the comparison of equilibria, there is no essential difference; so the difference must lie in a view about 'Traverse', about the route which the system is supposed to take from the one equilibrium to the other.

The quantity theory begins from a change in money supply; the wage theorem begins from a change in the level of money wages. If we begin from a change in the level of money wages, by what means are we to suppose that the new equilibrium is established? It should by now be clear (from what I said in my first lecture) that it will make a difference whether we make the flexprice hypothesis, according to which prices are determined by demand and supply, or the fixprice hypothesis, according to which demand and supply do not necessarily, in the short run, have to be equal. (Or whether we make the realistic hypothesis, that some markets are fixprice and some are flexprice.) Keynes, it seems to me, was usually, in this context, thinking in a fixprice manner; that, in any case, is how he seems usually to be interpreted. In a pure fixprice system, prices are likely to be fixed, in the short run, so as to cover normal costs; so when wages are raised, prices are likely to be raised correspondingly. This is realistic enough—one sees it happening. There is a complication, as Keynes saw, on the side of investment; I will come to that in a moment.

I think I may claim to have given, in my own *Value and Capital* (1939), the corresponding analysis for a flexprice system. It is not in Keynes; but it is needed, in order to complete what Keynes said.

As I showed in the first of these lectures, a fully flexprice system requires the presence of stockholding intermediaries, whose actions must be determined by their expectations of the movements of prices in the future. (These expectations are uncertain, but they may nevertheless be represented,

FCKE

sufficiently for most present purposes, by particular price-expectations.) It follows, almost obviously, that the wage-theorem can only hold in a pure flexprice system if there is unitary elasticity of these price-expectations (or static expectations—as Lange, perhaps more conveniently, was subsequently to call this condition). It is only if expected prices rise in the same proportion as current prices that the same *real* situation will be restored when the wage-level rises. If expected prices are based *solely* upon current prices that is what will happen. The flexprice system will then (but only then) react in the way we have been supposing the fixprice system to react.

Price-expectations do appear in Keynes's model, but only as affecting the marginal efficiency of capital—the expected rate of return on new investment. When money wages rise, the expected rate of return on marginal investment is supposed to remain unchanged; and that can only happen if the prices, at which output from such investment is expected to be sold when it is ready, rise in the same proportion as current prices have risen. It is hard to see any reason why this should happen, unless it is assumed that expected prices are based on current prices. So a unitary elasticity of expectations, or something corresponding to it, seems in fact to be implied in Keynes's version.

It must, however, be emphasized that unitary elasticity of expectations does not imply that prices, in the future, after the current disturbance, are expected to remain unchanged. We might have begun from a situation in which prices were expected to be rising, perhaps at a steady rate (and wages at a corresponding rate); there could still be unitary elasticity of expectations if the current rise in wages did not affect the *expected rate of price-rise*. For the ratios between expected prices and current prices would, by that condition, remain the same. But how could it be that a current rise in wages did not affect the expected rate of price-rise? Only, I think, if the current rise in wages was itself expected, if the system was already adjusted to that rise in wages *in advance*.

It is clearly possible, at least in principle, and at least in a flexprice system (this qualification, as we shall see, is important), that there might be full adjustment to inflationary rising wages, and correspondingly rising prices—an 'inflationary equilibrium', with no alteration in *real* price-ratios from what they would have been if there had been no inflation. The actual stage II system, as I previously described it, is clearly not an inflationary equilibrium in that sense; for it is not in equilibrium (fluctuations about equilibrium have not been abolished). But the inflationary equilibrium helps to explain what happens; it is useful, at the least, as a standard of reference.

Real price-ratios are the same, in inflationary equilibrium, whatever the rate of inflation; but the rate of interest, being a rate of exchange between money now and money in the future, is not one of these real price-ratios. In order that real price-ratios should be the same as they would have been without inflation, the money rate of interest must be adjusted for the expected fall in the value in money. So inflationary equilibrium implies high rates of money interest.

This fully accords with experience, and does not, I think, in this place require further discussion.

Inflationary equilibrium, as just defined, is an equilibrium in Keynes's sense; it does not imply that there is full employment. So suppose that we start from a state of inflationary equilibrium, in which there is much unemployment, and ask the critical question, What can be done about it? Is there any reason why the Keynesian prescription should not be applicable? Should we not still, in spite of the inflation, seek, by fiscal policy or by monetary policy, to raise the effective demand for labour?

The importance of the distinction which I drew, at the beginning of this lecture, between the three views about changes in money wages, at once becomes manifest. According as one takes one of these views or another, one will answer this critical question in different ways.

If one takes the first view—the 'radical' view—one will clearly, even in inflationary conditions, follow Keynes, the old Keynes. If one holds that wage-inflation has non-economic causes, its existence is no reason for not following the orthodox Keynesian policy; for the inflation will proceed, at much the same rate, whether the demand for labour is expanded or not. One can just avert one's eyes from the inflation, doing one's sums in constant prices! One will indeed arrive at the same conclusion, if one holds, on other grounds, that inflation does not matter. That, I suppose, is 'orthodox' Keynesianism; but (as we shall see) it averts its eyes from what are (now) important facts.

If one takes the second view—the Phillips view—the

verdict is very different. There is no doubt, on this view, that inflation does matter. But any measure which increases employment will aggravate inflation; so if the initial inflation is all we can bear, we must accept the initial employment. If we can stand a higher rate of inflation, we can diminish unemployment, but not otherwise.

As you will have gathered, I do not myself subscribe to either of these views. I do believe that inflation does matter, but I think one should start by explaining why.

To the ordinary man it is obvious that inflation matters; but the economist is unwise to take it for granted. For he can easily fall into a habit of mind in which it is not obvious at all. It is perfectly true that in a perfect flexprice economy (so useful to him as a tool of analysis) inflation does not matter—or hardly matters. If all prices are free to move, and all contracts can be offset if desired (as in a commodity market with forward dealing), dealers can allow for inflation in every contract that they make. Money is just a ticket; and the constancy of its value, over time, is a matter of little importance. There is just one sophisticated reason why it may be of some importance, a reason which has been brought to our attention by Milton Friedman[4] and other American economists, who (notoriously) live in their thinking in just such a world. The higher the rate of inflation, and (in consequence) the higher the rates of money interest, the greater will be the sacrifice involved in holding money instead of investing it in securities. Thus, even in inflationary equilibrium, less money will be held (relatively

[4] See his *Optimum Quantity of Money* (1969).

to the existing level of prices) than would have been held if prices had been stable, or the rate of inflation had been less. There is thus a loss of 'convenience and security' which is purely due to the inflation—a loss which remains after all other effects of inflation have been neutralized, as with a perfect forward market they can be. One must, I think, accept that there is, in principle, this 'Friedman' loss; but it seems to me to be a small loss compared with others, which arise from the fact that actual markets are not perfect flexprice markets.

In fixprice markets, prices have to be 'made'; they are not just determined, from day to day, by demand and supply. This applies, most of all, to markets for labour, where wages have to be negotiated; but it also applies to fixprice markets of many other kinds. The only markets to which it does not apply are speculative markets, such as markets for staple commodities and markets for securities; these do indeed behave in Friedman's fashion. Now wherever prices have to be made, there is a question how they shall be made. It is much easier to make them, in a way which seems satisfactory to the parties concerned (because it seems fair), if substantial use can be made of precedent; if one can at least start the bargaining from some presumption that what has been acceptable before will be acceptable again. When prices in general are fairly stable, that is often rather easy. The particular prices which result from such bargains may not be ideal from the point of view of the economist; but the time and trouble which would be involved in improving them is simply not worth while. To be obliged to make them anew, and to go on making them anew, as one is obliged to do in continuous inflation, involves loss—direct economic loss, and (very often) loss of temper as well.

It is of course in the labour market that such considerations are of particular importance; but it is by no means only to the labour market that they apply. Any system of prices (a system of railway fares, just like a system of wage-rates) has to satisfy canons of economic efficiency *and* canons of fairness—canons which it is very difficult to make compatible. So it is bound to work more easily if it is allowed to acquire, to some degree, the sanction of custom—if it is not, at frequent intervals, being torn up by the roots.

This, I believe, is the true reason why inflation is damaging. It is most apparent in deterioration of industrial relations; but it is not confined to that field—it extends much more widely. It extends, very importantly, to many kinds of public arrangements—pensions and social benefits on the one hand, taxes and fines on the other. In conditions of inflation these continually need re-fixing, so that issues which had seemed closed have to be reopened. All this is left out in the perfect flexprice model; but these are the ways in which inflation really hurts.

I return, in the light of these considerations, to what I have called the critical question: if there is inflation, and unemployment, how far does the Keynesian prescription stand? We cannot, I think it can now be seen, give a simple answer. We shall agree with the 'Phillips' school that inflation is an evil, just as unemployment is an evil; but we shall not follow them in their pessimism—we shall not be sure that *anything* which alleviates unemployment must aggravate inflation. We shall not even be sure that to alleviate unemployment by fiscal or monetary expansion *must* make inflation worse. We shall want to look very carefully at the *ways* in which it may aggravate inflation—in particular, wage-inflation.

It would appear, from what has been said, that there are at least two ways in which this may happen, quite different ways, which need to be distinguished. One is that which we have associated with the 'Phillips theory'. Particular scarcities of labour appear ahead of general scarcity, so that there is a rise in particular wages (from demand-pull) in excess of the rise which would have occurred without the expansionary policy. Once this occurs on any considerable scale, it is likely (for the reasons I have stated) to be generalized; so that there will be a general wage-inflation in excess of what would have been experienced otherwise. That is one possibility which must be faced. It is nevertheless not inevitable that *any* expansion must have a significant effect of this sort. An expansion which is strongly biased towards expanding demand for kinds of labour which are, initially, not over-plentiful will have a much more serious effect than one which is better balanced.

The other way, in which expansion may aggravate inflation, is quite different—and probably, to judge from recent experience, more important. I took much trouble, in my first lecture, to distinguish between the case in which the non-labour resources which are needed to support expansion are fairly abundant (the case which, I believe, Keynes himself had mainly in mind) and the case in which expansion encounters non-labour shortages. In a closed economy, as I explained, this distinction is mainly a matter of the availability of stocks, of materials and of finished goods; but in an open economy, the economy of a single nation, it is usually, first of all, a question of foreign exchange. For exchange reserves are of all stocks the easiest on which to draw. But it is of the greatest importance to insist that the issue, in each case, is basically the same.

Take first the closed economy. If the goods of which shortages develop are traded on fixprice markets, their prices need not respond to the shortages; demands will go unsatisfied, order books will lengthen, but that is all. But in any economy where flexprice markets are important, excess demand is likely to percolate to those flexprice markets, and in those markets excess demand must lead to a rise in price. A rise in the prices of materials, if it is expected to be short-lived, need not raise the prices of the finished goods incorporating those materials; for these finished goods will often be sold on fixprice markets, prices which depend on normal costs, not (so much) on the costs of the moment. Some of the prices of finished goods will surely, however, fairly soon be affected; and in the case of foodstuffs, they are likely to be affected quite rapidly. Now a rise in the prices of consumer goods (as we have seen) is particularly likely to aggravate wage-inflation. I have tried to state this sequence in such a way as to make clear that it does not necessarily happen. But it is one of the things which in a considerable expansion is very likely to happen; so it is one of the things against which the exponents of an expansionary policy need to be on their guard.

I turn to the open economy, on which there is much more to be said—more than can possibly be said at the end of these lectures. I must keep to the main point.

If a country has external reserves, on which it can draw freely, and if it is able to acquire additional imports at prices which are substantially unaffected by its additional demand for them (so that imports behave like fixprice commodities), it will be quite free, so long as these conditions last, from the trouble we have just been discussing. It is indeed almost inconceivable that so favourable a conjunction will last indefinitely, but it may last long enough. For the excess demand for imports need not be more than temporary; it is possible that increased production at home may replace imports, or may make available additional exports, by which the extra imports can be paid for. It will, however, inevitably take time for this to happen; and increased production must be in a suitable form if it is to happen at all. It will not necessarily happen, even after delay, with *any* expansionary programme.

Suppose, on the other hand, that there are no external reserves, or that they are very limited. Imports are then not available to provide the relief that is required. The position is basically similar to that of the closed economy. (It is perhaps a little better than that of the actual closed economy, since particular scarcities can be relieved by imports, at the cost of aggravating other scarcities; the latter, however, may be less acute.) In general, however, the analogy holds. It is impossible to overcome the constraint by exchange depreciation, since this simply means that imports are made to behave like flexprice commodities; excess demand leads to a rise in import prices, and hence (via consumer goods) to aggravation of inflation.

Consider what happens when the first of these cases passes over to the second. There have been sufficient reserves to support an expansion in its early stages; but without the point being reached at which the expansion becomes 'self-sustaining', the reserves are exhausted (and cannot be supplemented by foreign borrowing). The country is then in the dire position that its current level of employment, *and* its current level of real wages, are levels that it cannot sustain, cannot possibly sustain. Something has to give. It may be possible, by desperate efforts, to avoid exchange depreciation; but that cannot be done unless the expansion is cut back severely; the whole of the shock must then be taken by employment. Exchange depreciation diminishes that shock, but at the cost of aggravating inflation, the natural response (we shall now understand) to a cut in real wages. But since inflation is an ineffective way of cutting real wages, some part of the shock will still have to be borne by employment. Thus, as a result of the crisis, there is exchange depreciation, increased inflation, and rising unemployment, all (more or less) at the same time.

I am thinking, of course, of the British experience in 1967–70 and again in 1972–3. The trouble, however, is quite general; any country which pursues an active employment policy will have to take care if it is not to experience the same trouble.

I conclude with some general reflections. Keynesian economics, when reformulated in the light of modern experience, is a much less cheerful subject than it appeared to be at first, in its glad dawn of 1936. It can no longer say to the statesman *'Fays ce que vouldras'*—you will be right to do just what you would like to do, what will earn you popularity if you do it. The task is much harder than that. I would nevertheless insist that the revised version, which I have tried to give, is descended from Keynes's; we could not understand the problems which confront us today, as well as we can now do, without making much use of what Keynes has given us. Reformulated Keynes is much more like Keynes than it is like the cruder forms of 'neo-classical' doctrine. It should nevertheless borrow some thoughts from Keynes's fellow-workers, such as Pigou and Robertson, from whom he separated himself (overmuch, one would now think) in 1936. For the awareness, which they had, that mere expansion, without attention to the control of fluctuation, is insufficient, is one of the things we have to recover.

There is another way also in which the task is now seen to be harder. I may have given the impression, in the preceding, that all would be well if prices (and wages) were more stable; so that fixprice markets, because they make, even to a limited extent, for stability, have positive merits. I think that they do have this merit; but I am fully aware that they have grievous demerits on the other side. I am maintaining that it is part of the business of the economist to keep in mind the issues I have been discussing—that he should always be aware, very fully aware, that prices have a social function as well as an allocative function. But they do have an allocative function; to have elucidated that allocative function is one of the principal achievements of economics. I am not in the least implying that we should abandon all we have learned in that direction. We must hold fast to that too. We should indeed appreciate that a world in which optimum efficiency is attainable through free use of a price-mechanism is very far off. That is nevertheless no reason why we should not continually be exerting ourselves to look for practical ways of improving economic efficiency—sub-optimizing, as it is sometimes called. This is as much a part of our duty, as the other.

At the conclusion of my first article on money,[5] published in 1935, a year before the *General Theory*—the paper in which I first looked round the corner at the new world which Keynes was to open up—I said that it offered 'the economist a pretty hard life, for he will not be able to have a clear conscience either way, over many of the alternatives he is called upon to consider. His ideals will conflict and he will not be able to seek an easy way out by sacrificing either.'

By that, after all, I still stand.

[5] 'A Suggestion for Simplifying the Theory of Money', *Economics*, 1935, reprinted in *Critical Essays*.